DO YOU REALLY WANT TO MEET IGUANODON?

BY ANNETTE BAY PIMENTEL • ILLUSTRATED BY DANIELE FABBRI

AMICUS ILLUSTRATED and AMICUS INK
are published by Amicus
P.O. Box 1329, Mankato, MN 56002
www.amicuspublishing.us

EDITOR: Alissa Thielges
SERIES DESIGNER: Kathleen Petelinsek
BOOK DESIGNER: Veronica Scott

LIBRARY OF CONGRESS CATALOGING-IN-PUBLICATION DATA
Names: Pimentel, Annette Bay, author. | Fabbri, Daniele,
   1978- illustrator.
Title: Do you really want to meet iguanodon? / by Annette
   Bay Pimentel ; illustrated by Daniele Fabbri.
Description: Mankato, Minnesota : Amicus Illustrated
   and Amicus Ink, [2020] | Series: Do you really want to
   meet a dinosaur? | Audience: K to grade 3. | Includes
   bibliographical references.
Identifiers: LCCN 2018041150 (print) | LCCN 2018043548
   (ebook) | ISBN 9781681517933 (pdf) | ISBN 9781681517117
   (library binding) | ISBN 9781681524979 (pbk.) |
Subjects: LCSH: Iguanodon--Juvenile literature. | Dinosaurs-
   -Juvenile literature.
Classification: LCC QE862.065 (ebook) | LCC QE862.065
   P55845 2020 (print) | DDC 567.914--dc23
LC record available at https://lccn.loc.gov/2018041150

Printed in the United States of America
HC 10 9 8 7 6 5 4 3 2 1
PB 10 9 8 7 6 5 4 3 2 1

ABOUT THE AUTHOR
Annette Bay Pimentel lives in Moscow, Idaho with her family.
She doesn't have a time machine, so she researches the
past at the library. She writes about what happened a
long time ago in nonfiction picture books like *Mountain Chef*
(2016, Charlesbridge). You can visit her online at
www.annettebaypimentel.com.

ABOUT THE ILLUSTRATOR
Daniele Fabbri was born in Ravenna, Italy, in 1978. He
graduated from Istituto Europeo di Design in Milan,
Italy, and started his career as a cartoon animator,
storyboarder, and background designer for animated
series. He has worked as a freelance illustrator since 2003,
collaborating with advertising agencies and international
publishers, including many books for Amicus.

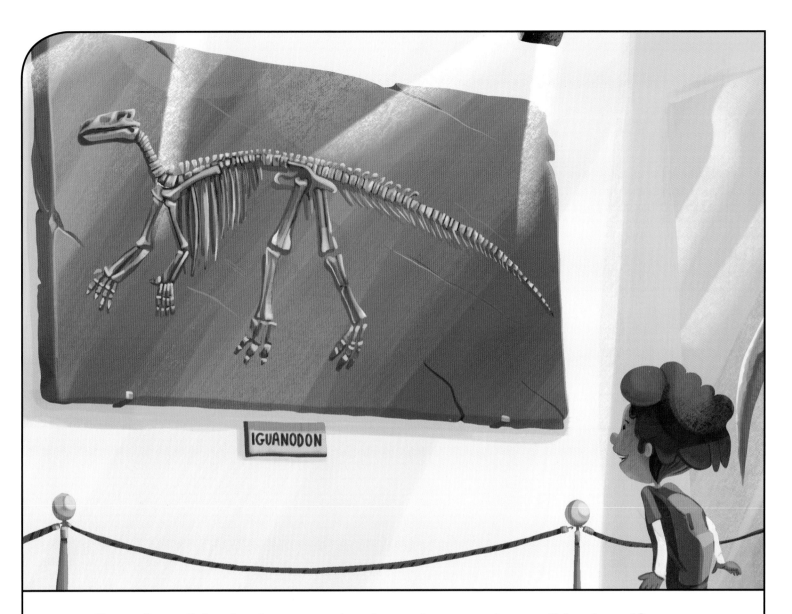

That fossil looks impressive hanging on the wall by itself.
But in real life Iguanodons lived in groups. Wouldn't you love
to see an Iguanodon herd?

Iguanodons lived in Belgium 125 million years ago. But now they are extinct. You'll need to travel back in time. Find a time machine. Set it for the early Cretaceous Period—and head for western Europe.

It's hot and dry when you arrive. But you see dark clouds. Maybe rain is coming.

Iguanodon shouldn't be hard to spot. Many fossils of this large herbivore have been found around here. Follow the plants they like to munch on.

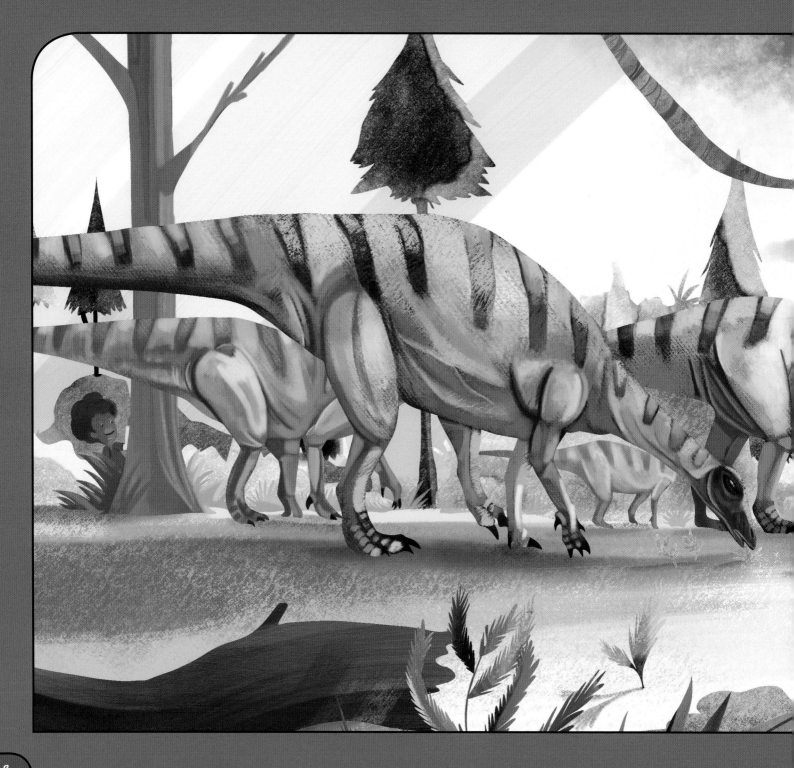

You found a herd! Sticking together protects Iguanodons from meat-eaters. The Iguanodon's size scares away some predators, too. It's big! It stretches 30 feet (9 m) long and stands 13 feet (4 m) tall. That's as long as 3 cows and taller than 2 grown men.

Don't let Iguanodon step on your foot. It weighs 11,000 pounds (4,989 kg). That's as much as an elephant! Climb a tree to keep safe.

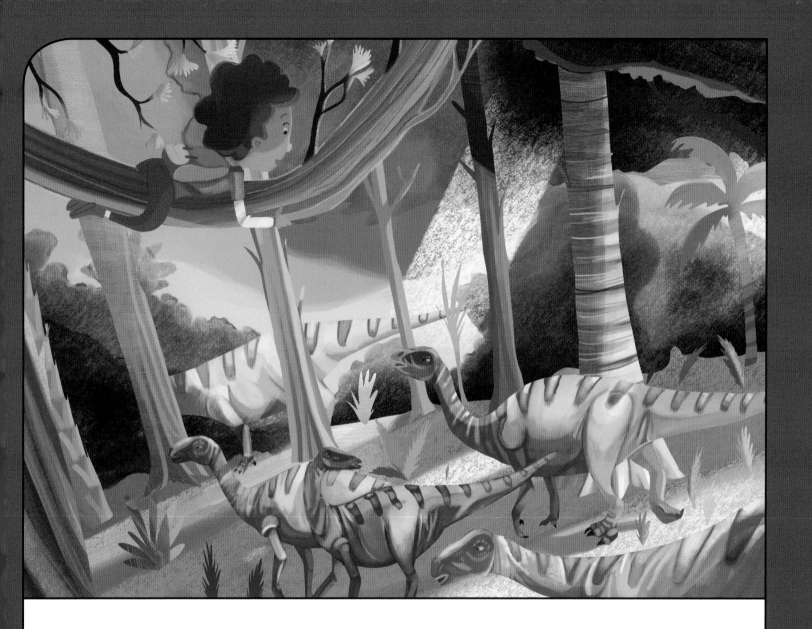

Even up here you can't tell which are male and which are female.

But the Iguanodons somehow know the difference!

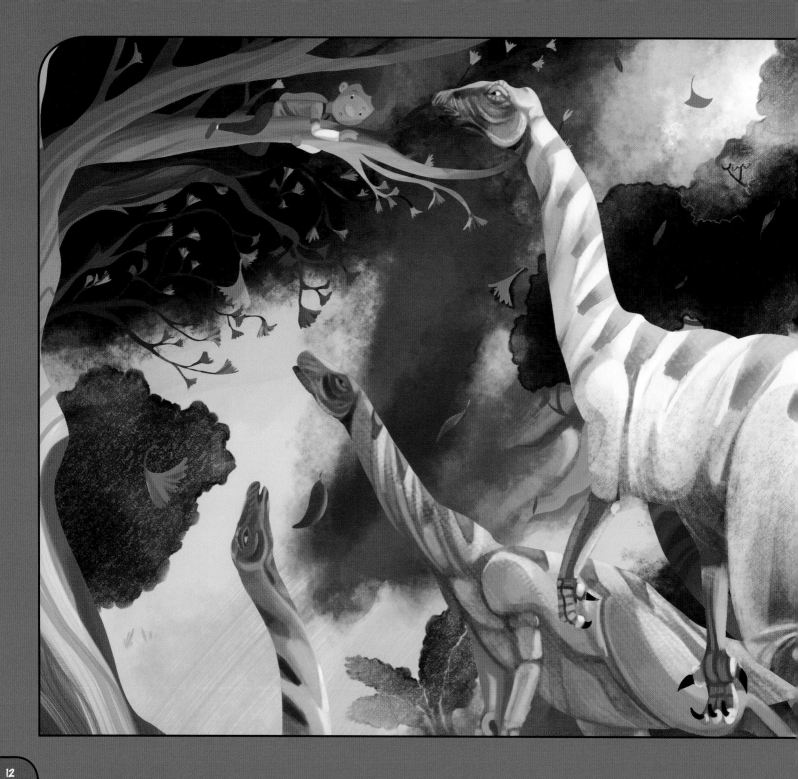

Iguanodons can walk on either all four legs or just two. Now, a group rears up on two legs. One nudges you with its head. It's looking for something to munch on up here in the tree. Don't worry, it only eats plants. You're not on the menu.

Avoid that thumb! It's sharp and tough. It looks like a spike. Scientists aren't sure how Iguanodon uses it. It may help Iguanodon strip leaves off trees or break open tough seeds.

Crack! Lightning strikes nearby.

You're in for a storm.

The dinosaurs shuffle uneasily. Are they sniffing the air? Iguanodon has a great sense of smell. What does it smell now? Smoke!

You see flames. The lightning struck a tree! A wildfire roars.

Climb down. The herd will lead you to safety.

The Iguanodons find a lake. Standing in water, they may be safe from the fire. You start to follow. Mud sucks at your shoe. Oh no! This is no normal lake. This is quicksand! The Iguanodons will have a hard time getting out. You would, too. Go no further!

You can't do anything to help the Iguanodon herd. But you can escape the fire. Hurry back to your time machine and head home. You'll always have the memory of the day you spent time with an Iguanodon herd.

GLOSSARY

Cretaceous Period—The time between 145.5 million and 65.5 million years ago. Dinosaurs lived during this time.

extinct—No longer found living anywhere in the world; known only from other fossils.

fossil—A bone or other trace of an animal from a long time ago, preserved as rock.

herbivore—An animal that only eats plants.

herd—A group of animals that feed and travel together.

predators—Animals that hunt other animals for food.

quicksand—An area of sand or soil so saturated with water that it cannot support anything standing on its surface.

AUTHOR'S NOTE

Time machines aren't real, of course. But the details about Iguanodon in this book are based on research by scientists who study fossils. In 1878, 38 Iguanodon skeletons were dug up in a coal mine in Belgium. But it wasn't until 2012 that researchers figured out that those dinosaurs probably died in quicksand. New dinosaur discoveries are made every year. Look up the books and websites below to learn more.

READ MORE

Gilbert, Sara. *Iguanodon*. Mankato, Minn.: Creative Education, 2019.

Hirsch, Rebecca E. *Iguanodon*. Mendota Heights, Minn.: Focus Readers, 2018.

Riehecky, Janet. *Iguanodon and Other Bird-Footed Dinosaurs: The Need-to-Know Facts*. North Mankato, Minn.: Capstone, 2017.

WEBSITES

DINOSAUR GALLERY
https://www.naturalsciences.be/en/museum/exhibitions-view/239/394/390
Watch a video about the discovery of Iguanodon fossils in 1878.

IGUANODON FACTS FOR KIDS
http://www.sciencekids.co.nz/sciencefacts/dinosaurs/iguanodon.html
Read cool facts on Iguanodon.

PBS KIDS: DINOSAUR GAMES
https://pbskids.org/games/dinosaur/
Play games to learn more about these extinct animals.

Every effort has been made to ensure that these websites are appropriate for children. However, because of the nature of the Internet, it is impossible to guarantee that these sites will remain active indefinitely or that their contents will not be altered.